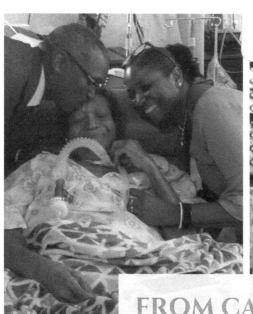

FROM CAREFREE
TO CAREGIVER

A 31 DAY DEVOTIONAL TO
BALANCE, SUPPORT, AND
STRENGTHEN YOU IN YOUR
NEW ROLE

TERALEEN R. CAMPBELL

Written By: Teraleen R. Campbell © 2018
www.teraleencampbell
Published By: Pen Legacy®
Editor: Laura Charles-Horne
Cover Design: DeShon Gales, DG Creative Studio
Formatting By: The Liar's Craft

Scriptures marked KJV are taken from the KING JAMES VERSION (KJV): KING JAMES VERSION, public domain.

Scripture quotations are taken from the Holy Bible, New Living Translation, copyright ©1996, 2004, 2015 by Tyndale House Foundation. Used by permission of Tyndale House Publishers, Inc., Carol Stream, Illinois 60188. All rights reserved.

Library of Congress Cataloging – in- Publication Data has been applied for.

ISBN: 978-0-692-11593-0

PRINTED IN THE UNITED STATES OF AMERICA.

Dedication

This is dedicated to the memory of my beloved mother. This is my God-inspired way to chronicle and honor the final years of our journey together. I thank the Lord for selecting me to be your daughter. I am ever mindful of the fact that I am the beneficiary of your prayers.

I also dedicate this to every person who is currently on the caregiving journey. Please know that I am praying for you. May the pages of this book cause you to be lifted and renewed as you journey on.

Journaling has been a great source of refuge and strength along my caregiving journey. Therefore, pages have been included for you journal or take notes after each passage. I encourage you to take advantage of the space. You will find it beneficial to your emotional and spiritual well-being.

Foreword

God allows us to cross paths with people in various ways and for various reasons. Connecting with Teraleen Campbell was part of God's divine plan. Like Teraleen, I had the honor of caring for my beloved mother during her final years. While not easy, I cherish each day that I was able to spend with her. I can truly say that I would not trade those moments for anything.

Teraleen is a servant leader who has a heart for people and for prayer. Also like me, she wears multiple hats. While leading others, she has had to step away from the public view of ministry in order to fulfill her responsibilities as a loving daughter caring for her mother. I personally know too well that this is no easy task.

In the pages of this book, Teraleen parts the curtains of her life and provides insight, not to the various public roles that she fulfills, rather to the most important one, the daughter who cared for her mother during the final years of her life. I appreciate her willingness to be open and share some private aspects of her journey.

During my time as International President of Zeta Phi Beta Sorority, Inc., Elder Care was one of my signature service projects. For me and my family, Elder Care was personal. With that in mind, I decided to make positive impact on the lives of seniors and their families, many of whom were caregivers.

As caregivers, we give of ourselves in many ways: financially, physically, and emotionally. Therefore, time to refresh ourselves is necessary. This devotional has been designed to be a tool that will strengthen you along your caregiving journey.

I believe that this book will fill a void for many. I know too well the internal conflict that goes along with being a caregiver.

Although one feels a sense of love and admiration toward the person for whom they provide care, they also grow tired and weary at times. Yes, I understand these range of emotions. Some days are good, while others leave something to be desired. There are days when the weight of this new way of life become overwhelming. It will be especially during those times when the passages of this book will be tremendously valuable.

From Carefree to Caregiver has been written by a caregiver for caregivers. Having walked the caregiving journey myself, I have a strong sense of compassion for those who give of themselves to care for others. It is not a chore. It is a labor of love.

What I find most beneficial and unique is that Teraleen had the forethought not only to share parts of her journey with her mother, but to do so in a devotional form. Having been the recipient of her ministry of prayer, I am confident that each prayer has been thoughtfully written, and that each passage of scripture will speak to you as you read.

This is a devotional that will speak to your heart and soul. It will meet you where you are and help you put your own caregiving journey into proper perspective. You will celebrate the victorious days, while finding strength on the days when you feel weak and finding courage during times when critical decisions must be made. In a nutshell, through this book, Teraleen shares her personal faith journey and walk with God; and shows how He is an integral part of walking victoriously through the caregiving journey.

May God bless you as you read From Carefree to Caregiver. May you be encouraged and uplifted. Moreover, may you feel a sense of renewed strength as you continue along your caregiving journey.

Dr. Mary Breaux Wright
24th International President
Zeta Phi Beta Sorority, Incorporated

From Carefree to Caregiver

Table of Contents

Caring Is A Blessing

I drove up to Hagerstown to take care of some business today. Of course, I also stopped by to see Mom. Since I hadn't spoken with her in advance, she wasn't aware of my visit.

Needless to say, she was happy to see me. She kept saying, "I didn't know you were coming." I just smiled. She was really happy that I had stopped by Popeyes and picked up a chicken dinner. Mom was glad that she didn't have to eat the nursing home food. Although it seemed like such a small thing, the fact that she was happy blessed me immensely. I realized that through all the ups and downs, there is a blessing in caring for a parent.

As I wrote on Facebook, the longer that the Lord allows my mother to live, it is my pleasure to serve her. I realize that she is the ONE person who sacrificed whatever possible so that I might have a good life. As my parent, I recognize that she once was my caregiver; therefore having the opportunity to care for her is a privilege and an honor.

Scripture - The generous will prosper; those who refresh others will themselves be refreshed. Proverbs 11:25 NLT

Prayer - Lord, I thank You for blessing me to be a blessing. If it were not for You, I would not be able to do the things that I do. I never want You to consider me as ungrateful. Quite the contrary, I am grateful that You bless me so that I may continue to bless others. I acknowledge the fact that it is You who has blessed me with the ability and means to be a caregiver. I thank you for every time that you allow positive interactions to remind me of the blessings that are also part of this journey. This is my prayer today, in Jesus' name. Amen!

Notes:

_____

_____

_____

_____

_____

_____

_____

_____

_____

_____

_____

_____

_____

_____

_____

_____

_____

_____

On The Job Training

This journey has been one that has brought humility, frustration, sadness, joy, praise, relief, and a host of other emotions. One of the initial emotions that I felt was fear – fear of the unknown. How am I supposed to do this? Will my mother's health improve? Will she remain unable to talk or walk? (She was blessed to regain ability to do both.) How much longer will God allow her to live? (Seven years.) How am I going to handle all that has been put upon me? (God's grace.) How will I afford this? (The Lord blessed me to do so.)

I really wish I had some advance notification that I would become a caregiver. There was none. I wish I could have been trained, taken a class, webinar, had a process map, outline, or something before being thrust into this role. Unfortunately, that is not quite the way that some things in life work. We cannot have each situation delivered to us in a nice, neat package.

It is in instances such as these when we should consider ourselves blessed to have a heavenly Father from whom we can seek wisdom and guidance. I have concluded that God is the ultimate trainer. When we ask Him for wisdom, He will provide on the job training. He prepares us for each and every test and trial that comes our way. He helps to ensure that the weapons and darts that are formed and thrown at us will not be successful. They will not take us out!

We can banish every feeling of inadequacy. We can cancel the notion that we don't know what we are doing. As long as we seek the Lord and apply the resources that are at our disposal, we will not fail!

Scripture - If you need wisdom, ask our generous God, and he will give it to you. He will not rebuke you for asking. But when you ask him, be sure that your faith is in God alone. Do not waver, for a person with divided loyalty is as unsettled as a wave of the sea that is blown and tossed by the wind. Such people should not expect to receive anything from the Lord. James 1:5-7 NLT

Prayer - I thank You, Lord, for being the ultimate teacher and trainer. I appreciate every time that Your Spirit has led me. I thank You for crowning me with wisdom. I do not take it for granted. I thank You for each lesson that You have allowed me to learn along my life's journey. Because of You, I can silence every voice that seeks to instill fear in me. Because of You, I know no defeat – only success! Again, I say, thank You, Lord! In Jesus' name, Amen!

Notes:

_____

_____

_____

_____

_____

_____

_____

_____

_____

_____

_____

_____

_____

_____

_____

_____

_____

_____

But God

Today marks the final weekend of the year. It's somewhat surreal that we've come to this point already. As I look over the past 362 days, I must pause and say thank you, Jesus! We've lost two members of our family, both suddenly, leaving some reeling, but God has kept us. But God!

Some members of the family were diagnosed with illnesses yet they remain. Finances were sketchy, but God provided. My best friend was hospitalized for 2 months, but God healed her! My mother was sent to the hospital four times this year, but God brought her out each time!

No matter what is going on in your life, I encourage you to think back on what did *not* happen. Rehearse in your mind how the Lord changed what appeared to be a no-win, dismal situation into one of overcoming. Remember, the storms that came in your life; however, God did not allow them to consume you. Once you do this, offer up a But God Praise! We've had some struggles – *but God* brought us through them! Trust me when I say, you will then have strength to go on.

Scripture - This I recall to my mind; therefore have I hope. It is of the Lord's mercies that we are not consumed, because his compassions fail not. They are new every morning: great is thy faithfulness. Lamentations 3:21-23 KJV

Prayer - Father, today, I take time to thank You for preserving me. I thank You for keeping me through it all. Yes, there have been difficult days, but You have kept us. We can truly say, if it had not been for You on our side, we do not know where we would be. Thank you for not allowing us to be consumed. Thank you for being a faithful Creator! In Jesus' name, Amen!

Notes:

_____

_____

_____

_____

_____

_____

_____

_____

_____

_____

_____

_____

_____

_____

_____

_____

An Advocate

In the early stages of this journey, I realized that my role as a caregiver would include being an advocate for my mother. Believe me when I say, it was mentally and emotionally draining, yet absolutely necessary!

I saw so many questionable occurrences in hospitals and nursing homes that it was almost unreal. Early on, there was a nurse who wanted my family to give up on my mother, saying she would never regain any quality of life. Boy was she wrong! I have come to understand that healthcare really is a business. Sometimes, patients and residents get caught between the mission of patient care and the profit and loss aspect of the industry. I believe that some nurses and physicians forget they are dealing with people's lives.

I've been a first-hand witness to some of the most caring healthcare professionals. In particular, one nursing aide who took her own money to purchase personal care items for my mother's roommate, since the women's family never visited. I prayed a special blessing upon her.

Thankfully, my mother spent a large part of her career working in healthcare. Therefore, she was well aware of her rights. She would call me in a heartbeat, if she felt they had been violated. I thanked the Lord daily that my mother retained the ability to speak during her 6-year nursing home stay. I covered her cell phone bill for this very reason. I prayed earnestly for residents who could not communicate with family members.

There were countless times when I had to advocate for my mother. I reported both hospital and nursing home staff for misconduct. I periodically took week days off from work in order to make the drive and do surprise visits to my mother. I often heard the staff walk down the hall and tell coworkers, "Cindy's daughter is here." Yes, I wanted them to know that I and my family or friends may show up at any time and my mom needed to be well taken care of whenever we arrived.

I moved my mother from one nursing facility that consistently provided substandard care. I have had interactions with patient advocates at the local hospital as well as the nursing home ombudsman. I am grateful for friends who are medical professionals. They provided valuable advice and guidance as well as helped to retain my faith in the healthcare system.

Scripture - Speak up for those who cannot speak for themselves; ensure justice for those being crushed. Yes, speak up for the poor and helpless, and see that they get justice. Proverbs 31:8-9 NLT; And I will ask the Father, and he will give you another Advocate, who will never leave you. John 14:16 NLT

Prayer - Dear Heavenly Father, today I thank You for giving me the ability to navigate through the healthcare system. I ask that You help me make sound decisions on behalf of my family. I praise You for healthcare professionals who go the extra mile as they care for others. I ask kind Father that You infuse a spirit of compassion into those who need it. I take time to pray a hedge of protection around patients and residents in hospitals and nursing homes. This is my prayer. In Jesus' name, Amen!

Notes:

_____

_____

_____

_____

_____

_____

_____

_____

_____

_____

_____

_____

_____

_____

_____

_____

_____

_____

_____

_____

_____

One Of Those Days

Today has not been the best day. I'm honestly feeling overwhelmed and quite exhausted. I am beyond drained. Between inquiries from people and dealing with the mere thought that I may lose someone I love, it's becoming a bit overwhelming.

I know that people do mean well. However, I wish they would realize that they are generally not the only ones who have questions. Answering the same questions multiple times is emotionally exhausting. I also wish they would respect my privacy and understand the sheer drain that can result during these times.

Having to deal with your own emotions then shifting into business mode and handling the personal affairs of someone else can be a daunting task. Good grief! It's hard enough to take care of your own bills and personal business at times. Going through papers and files, trying to locate whatever is necessary to complete yet another application; then, faxing or sending such documents to the appropriate party can be tedious, time consuming and downright tiring. If the healthcare and livelihood of my mom were not connected to retrieving those documents, sometimes I think I would say "forget it."

There are days when I have barely been able to get out of the bed as a result of feeling physically or emotionally exhausted. But God has continued to send strength from on high!

One assurance is that the Lord promised not to put more on us than we can bear.

Scripture - Each time he said, "My grace is all you need. My power works best in weakness." So now I am glad to boast about my weaknesses, so that the power of Christ can work through me. 2 Corinthians 12:9 NLT

Prayer - Father, today, I come truly as an empty pitcher before a full fountain. I ask You to refill, restore and replenish the areas in my spirit that are lacking. I place myself in Your hands and humbly ask You to send the strength needed to handle the assignment of this season in my life. I do know that all things continue to be possible with You. I thank You in advance for renewing my strength. In Jesus' name, amen!

Notes:

_____

_____

_____

_____

_____

_____

_____

_____

_____

_____

_____

_____

_____

_____

_____

_____

_____

_____

Keep Calm

The nursing home just called to inform me that Mom is having trouble breathing and is being sent to the ER. The nurse also said that Mom doesn't want to go. After immediately going into warfare prayer, I called and spoke with Mom. She is indeed struggling to get air, but is not up to all that goes along with a hospital visit. I talked calmly to her to reassure her that things will be fine.

My fellow caregivers will understand the sheer anxiety that can come over you upon getting this type of phone call. If you are like me, you immediately must go into prayer in order to calm your own nerves and remove anxiety. I go into prayer because I know that my mind and spirit need to be free and clear to make sound decisions, if necessary. Additionally, I know that my mom needs me to provide emotional support. Lastly, from a spiritual perspective, I am mindful that it is Satan's good pleasure to disrupt my thoughts and get them off kilter. Such can lead to feeling overwhelmed and to feelings of helplessness.

Recognizing that this is also a spiritual battle, I go into warfare prayer, binding the works of the wicked one in addition to any demonic influences that may be at work. When all is said and done, I have to trust and believe that God has His hand on her.

Scripture - For I know the one in whom I trust, and I am sure that he is able to guard what I have entrusted to him until the day of his return. 2 Timothy 1:12 NLT

Prayer – Father, I come tonight knowing that You have Your hand on my loved one. I ask You to be with her right now in a way that I cannot. I ask You to guide the intellect of the medical staff. Touch every doctor, nurse and technician who will come in contact with her. I know You to be an omniscient God, who knows what is happening, even when I do not. I also know You are an omnipresent God, who can provide calm and stability while I am unable to be there. I know you to be an omnipotent God, who has the power to keep things under control. I thank You so much for being a stabilizing force in this situation. In Jesus' name, I pray. Amen!

Notes:

_____

_____

_____

_____

_____

_____

_____

_____

_____

_____

_____

_____

_____

_____

_____

_____

_____

_____

_____

_____

_____

On The Bright Side

I admit that I am a little bummed. I haven't been able to get home to see my mommy for over a month. I've had vehicle issues and full weekend schedules that have prohibited me from getting to see her. I really feel guilty because I don't want her to think that I am deserting her. She's remained so positive and told me that she really wants me to get more rest, so that helps.

People have no idea how incredibly difficult it is to be the primary caregiver. The fact that the I don't live in the same local area, multiplies the challenge. While I am grateful for the support of my family, there are some things that I solely need to do.

I am grateful that the hand of the Lord is upon both of us, especially now. I thank Him for keeping His hand of protection on both of us. I thank Him that Mom is doing reasonably well. The fact that she's regained some mobility and is working on the hobby of crocheting helps a great deal.

Every now and then I want to just shout, "Look where He's brought her from!"

Scripture - Nay, in all these things we are more than conquerors through him that loved us. Romans 8:37 KJV

Prayer - Thank you for helping me to put my circumstances into proper perspective, Lord. Although the not-so-positive weighs on me, I am encouraged by the fact that there is a bright side. I bless You for illuminating the bright beyond the darkness. I praise You for the improvements that are taking place. Most of all, I thank and praise You for giving us the spirit of a conqueror! All things indeed do come of Thee and we thank Thee. In Jesus' name, Amen!

Notes:

_____

_____

_____

_____

_____

_____

_____

_____

_____

_____

_____

_____

_____

_____

_____

_____

_____

_____

A Sign

I took off work in order to attend an in-person Care Plan Meeting with the staff at the nursing home. Although I usually conduct these meetings via conference call, I opted to handle this one in person.

Not only was the meeting productive, but I was able to witness my mother walk down the hall! I was able to see my mom walk from her room down the hall about 30 steps. In fact, she walked past the next room! It was simply amazing to see Mom walking nearly three years after she became seriously ill. It is so true that our God is never, ever short of His word! That which He hath spoken, He is able and will perform.

The Unit Manager admitted that she really didn't think last year that Mom would really progress to the point of walking. She credited the physical therapy staff. While I am certainly thankful for them, I must also give God the glory! Just as we ask Him for help when we pray, we will give Him glory and praise when He answers those prayers. Again, I say, God gets the glory!

Scripture - For everything comes from him and exists by his power and is intended for his glory. All glory to him forever! Romans 11:36 NLT

Prayer - Lord, today I take time to thank you for giving me a sign and reminding me that it is not over. Thank You for giving me enough to continue to hold on. Words cannot adequately convey my level of gratitude. The best that I can do is continue to give You the Glory and honor that is due unto You.

Notes:

_____

_____

_____

_____

_____

_____

_____

_____

_____

_____

_____

_____

_____

_____

_____

_____

Step By Step

I had a successful care plan meeting with my mother's social worker and unit manager. Although last week was difficult for her, the meeting was successful. We all gained new understandings on how to proceed.

As a caregiver, it is important to go into meetings prepared. By that I mean, try remain level headed and not to become too emotional when handling business. I suggest jotting down some talking points for yourself prior to the meeting. This will help to ensure you stay on track, especially as healthcare professionals will likely bring up other topics for discussion. Doing so, also helps to ensure that you cover everything that you set out to discuss. I also suggest that you take notes during meetings with staff. This will help you keep track of items and follow-up to ensure completion.

I was informed during the meeting that Mom had progressed beyond physical therapy and is now part of what is called restorative therapy. After today's meeting, I was able to see her walk! I had not seen her walk in three years! My mom is simply amazing! She has overcome so much. I could barely contain myself as I watched her walk with her walker. Talk about being overcome with joy!

Mom did not take just a few steps. She walked from her room all the way down the hall. Thank you, Jesus! As the old Saints sang, "If you make one step, God will make two."

Scripture - "And I am sure of this, that He who began a good work in you will bring it to completion at the day of Jesus Christ." Philippians 1:6

Prayer - Lord, I thank You today for each step that is made toward total healing and restoration. I understand that progress is made when we don't remain stagnant, but with forward movement. I thank You for the intellect and knowledge to communicate with the healthcare staff. I ask that You touch them and keep them committed to the true mission of healthcare and healing.

Notes:

_____

_____

_____

_____

_____

_____

_____

_____

_____

_____

_____

_____

_____

_____

_____

_____

Between Faith And Fear

There are days when your faith is extremely high. There are also days when your faith is indifferent. While this may not seem to be problematic, the Lord tells us that lukewarm faith does not please him.

We must acknowledge the fact that life's pressures as well as its ups and downs can render us lukewarm at times. When this happens, we must fight to rekindle the fire that burns inside our souls, and make sure it burns for the things of God. In other words, we must fight to believe God again. We must fight for our faith.

Do you still believe the Lord is able to do the impossible? I encourage you to recall what He has already done in your life. Allow the victories of the past to lift your faith to the level where you will believe Him for your next victory.

Sometimes the doctor's reports, diagnoses, etc. threaten to undermine one's faith. It can become overwhelming and frustrating. It can feel as though you are at an intersection on a highway. On one side there is faith, but on the other is fear. A choice must be made. I also envision a seesaw. Some days faith is higher, but on others, fear takes over. Your inner man says, "Lord, help me to choose wisely and correctly."

Scripture - "What do you mean, 'If I can'?" Jesus asked. "Anything is possible if a person believes." The father instantly cried out, "I do believe, but help me overcome my unbelief!" Mark 9:23-24 NLT

Prayer - Lord, I honestly do not want to teeter between belief and unbelief. My sincere desire is to walk in faith. Today my request is that you help my unbelief. Please help me when life's circumstances seem to overshadow my faith in You. Remind me of the wonderful history that we have and the marvelous works that You have previously performed. Please know that my faith and hope ultimately lie in You. In Jesus' name, Amen!

Notes:

_____

_____

_____

_____

_____

_____

_____

_____

_____

_____

_____

_____

_____

_____

_____

_____

More Than A Feeling

Truth be told, there are some days when you simply are not feeling it. Not only are you not feeling it, you are not feeling people. You are not feeling much of anything.

Alas, I am reminded that I have someone who is depending on me for their well-being. With that in mind, on many of those "not feeling it days," you will likely have to brush yourself off, put your own feelings on the shelf, and begin to move forward with your day.

On days such as this, I remember the words of the Apostle Paul in Philippians 4, "I can do all things through Christ who gives me strength." Allow me to add a more practical thought or affirmation. I've got this. You've got this! We can do this! We will be alright!

Scripture - God is our refuge and strength, always ready to help in times of trouble. Psalms 46:5 NLT

Prayer - Today, Lord, I seek fortitude and stamina. I ask You to help me to do all that has been assigned to my hands, especially on behalf of my loved one. I admit that my spirit is at a low point. I ask You to help me today. Give me today my daily bread. I put my trust in Your ability to take me through. In Jesus' name, Amen!

Notes:

_____

_____

_____

_____

_____

_____

_____

_____

_____

_____

_____

_____

_____

_____

_____

_____

Warning Signs

Although my mom had been overweight for years, it did not worry me - until 2006. My mom's walking became increasingly difficult due to issues with her knees. She worked at a local nursing home for several years. As her walking became slower and slower, she had to stop working and go on disability.

Due to limited mobility, Mom's weight increased further. On a few occasions, I tried to discuss my concern with her, to no avail. She would often become annoyed with me. I even had a close friend, who had weight loss surgery, speak with her about that as an option.

I accompanied her on doctor appointments, only to learn that she had been going to a clinic rather than an actual doctor's office. The person who saw her at the clinic was a nurse practitioner and not a doctor, as we both had believed. The level of care and medical advice was inadequate in my opinion. The practitioner had limitations. She also did not seem to be interested in identifying ways to improve my mother's health.

Fast forward four years. Mom had what should have been a routine surgery. However, there was a complication; and suddenly she was clinging to life. Lord, help me because this is a bit much! I know that I am not the only one who has encountered sudden changes in life. They are unsettling to say the least – but God! It is true that hindsight is 20/20. While this is an uneasy time, I do believe that God will send help. I even thank Him for the warning signs because they provide a bit of insight into the current situation.

Scripture - For I am the Lord your God who takes hold of your right hand and says to you, Do not fear; I will help you. Isaiah 41:13

Prayer - Father, I am so glad that I am able to be open and honest with You. I am grateful that I can share even my frustrations with You. Today, I take time to pray for myself as I travel this caregiving journey. I thank You both for the warnings, and for the reassurance in Your Word that tells me that I will get through this. Even on difficult days, I know that I do not have to fear because You will help me. I praise You even now for the help that You are sending my way, in Jesus' name. Amen!

Notes:

_____

_____

_____

_____

_____

_____

_____

_____

_____

_____

_____

_____

_____

_____

_____

_____

Speak Into The Atmosphere

I just returned home from the hospital and reflecting on my visit. As I read healing scriptures to my mother, the nurse said something very profound to me. She told me that not everyone who comes into the room says positive things. I was so struck by her statement that I asked her to repeat it. "Some people who come in here are not positive, Ma'am. It is good that you are reading her scriptures and praying." She went on to encourage me to continue doing what I was doing.

As she worked, I posted a page of healing scriptures on the window with a note asking future visitors to read a few passages. After reading scriptures, I began to pray and walk around the room praying the Word of God. While praying, it dropped into my spirit that I needed to pray the Word out loud into the atmosphere. As I did, I saw a peace come over Mom and her monitors showed that the previously high blood pressure was coming down! It went from 202 (systolic) to 163! I could not help but to rejoice. My prayer shifted to one of giving thanks to the Lord.

I believe that the key was speaking into the atmosphere. By that I mean, speaking God's Word aloud, binding sickness and infection, then calling forth angels into the room to war on Mom's behalf and to minister to her needs. Yes, our words do have power!

Once the peace of God entered the room, a spirit of thanksgiving took over. This gave way to begin thanking the Lord for what He had already done, while believing and anticipating the results and manifestation here on Earth for even greater.

Scripture - *And I will give unto thee the keys of the kingdom of heaven: and whatsoever thou shalt bind on earth shall be bound in heaven: and whatsoever thou shalt loose on earth shall be loosed in heaven. Matthew 16:19 KJV*

Prayer - Father, I thank You for the spiritual keys that You have given me. I am grateful for the authority that You have granted that allows me to speak into the atmosphere in the name of Your son, Jesus. Thank you for allowing me to shift the atmosphere in a room, to bring calm where there is chaos, and to bring peace and stability. Grant wisdom, I pray so that I may speak effectively and with proper authority. In Jesus' name, Amen!

Notes:

_____

_____

_____

_____

_____

_____

_____

_____

_____

_____

_____

_____

_____

_____

_____

_____

_____

Anticipating Results

A colleague shared some bad news regarding his mother's health. Doctors have stated that her body was shutting down. They have called in the hospice team to help make her comfortable.

This brought a similar experience to mind. I recall the doctor telling me how my mother's body had an infection and her major organs were not functioning properly. Oh, how I remember feeling a pit in my throat and my heart sinking at the thought of losing my beloved Mommy.

I recall begging the Lord not to take her, yet not wanting to be selfish and keep her here if it meant she would have no quality of life. I remember the intense struggle between my spirit and my intellect. The doctor said it did not look good, yet I felt as if I had to hold on to faith even as I held her hand during each hospital visit.

I began to rehearse part of the mantra of Mom's church *"speaking in faith and anticipating results."* Those words became so real to me. I also thought of the passage in scripture where the disciple said, "Lord help my unbelief."

It is like you are straddling between two thought processes. On one hand, you go into an early state of grief at the mere possibility that you may lose a loved one. Then there is remorse over what should have been said, missed holidays, etc. On the other hand, you are doing all you can to keep your spirit lifted and demonstrate to the Lord that you do indeed have faith in His healing power and ability. Alas, we must take steps necessary to remain firm in our faith as we await God's next move.

Scripture - Why am I discouraged? Why is my heart so sad? I will put my hope in God! I will praise him again - my Savior and my God! Psalms 42:11 NLT

Prayer - Dear Lord, I come today seeking Your strength to hold on to faith in Your power and ability to heal and deliver. I ask that You heal my loved one. While You are healing, please deliver me from fear and anxiety. Heal whether through medicine, surgery, or divine intervention. I declare my faith in Your ability to do what doctors do not believe can happen because You are the God of the impossible. I thank You in advance for what You are going to do. In Jesus' name, Amen!

Notes:

_____

_____

_____

_____

_____

_____

_____

_____

_____

_____

_____

_____

_____

_____

_____

_____

A Reason To Celebrate

This week I celebrated my birthday. While this may seem insignificant, I am very grateful that the Lord allowed me to be on this Earth for this time. This is significant because I am a caregiver and studies show that the quality of life for caregivers declines as they care for their loved ones.

As we take care of family members, the tendency is to sacrifice our own health and well-being along the way. Lord knows I, too, struggle in this area. As I learn and grow, my goal is to improve and live a more balanced life as I handle my increased responsibilities.

We are all a work in progress, but with the help of the Lord, we will be just fine. We will be better than fine. We will be victorious!

Scripture - For the glory of your name, O Lord, preserve my life. Psalms 143:11 NLT

Prayer – Lord, today I want to express my gratefulness to You for preserving me. You are indeed a keeper! I thank You so much for keeping me in the midst of the responsibilities that are part of my life. I am so very grateful for life, health and strength.

Notes:

_____

_____

_____

_____

_____

_____

_____

_____

_____

_____

_____

_____

_____

_____

_____

_____

_____

_____

Looking Back

This week marks my 44th year of life. Part of me laments the fact that my mom is unable to come down to celebrate with me. Don't get me wrong. I am super grateful that she is alive. I simply wish she could travel and be part of the celebration.

She used to come down and take me to dinner faithfully for my birthday. She would also call, if she could not make the trip. Our "thing" was that she would call at 12:15PM. Her rationale was that I wasn't born until after 12 noon. Since she was my mother, she would know. She explained that it wasn't actually my birthday until the afternoon. We both always chuckled at her explanation.

Sometimes, you simply look back and have to give God praise for the days and occasions that you were able to share in the past. It's a blessing to know that you redeemed the opportunities that God afforded you with those whom you love. I can truly say that I thank the Lord that I had a mother who supported me through everything. For every parade and band competition, she was present. For each time I was recognized in church or my sorority, my mom was in place; and for that, I am so very grateful. Good memories can be a great source of strength and comfort.

Scripture - *I will praise you, LORD, with all my heart; I will tell of all the marvelous things you have done. I will be filled with joy because of you. I will sing praises to your name, O Most High. Psalms 9:1 NLT*

Prayer - Thank you, Lord. Thank you, Lord. Thank you, Lord. I just want to thank You, Lord! On this day of celebration, Lord, I thank You for my life. I thank You for the one who birthed me. Most of all, I thank You that my good days do indeed outweigh my bad days. I pray that you receive this prayer of thanksgiving. In Jesus' name, Amen!

Notes:

_____

_____

_____

_____

_____

_____

_____

_____

_____

_____

_____

_____

_____

_____

_____

_____

_____

_____

_____

Mother's Day

I'm so blessed to see another Mother's Day with my mother here alive and doing pretty well. Thank you, Lord, for keeping her body, mind and spirit for another year. We've both had our ups and downs; but through it all, the Lord has been more than faithful!

On this Mother's Day, my mind goes back to the myriad of sacrifices that my mother has made for me. I am sure that she has made numerous sacrifices that she never mentioned to me.

I thank and praise the Lord for my mommy: the nurse when I was sick, the defender when I was attacked and maligned, and the advocate when I did not have the courage to speak up for myself. Considering all of this, I count it an honor for our roles to somewhat be reversed. I've become a caregiver for her, a defender against those who would take advantage of her, and an advocate within this healthcare system that is sometimes difficult to navigate.

Yes, there are days when I am mentally and physically overwhelmed, but I would not have it any other way. I promised my mother when she first became ill that as long as she wanted to fight, I would be alongside her doing the same and take up the charge where she could not. God be my helper, I intend to remain true to that promise because my mother certainly has fought for me more times than I can count.

Scripture - "Honor your father and mother. Then you will live a long, full life in the land the Lord your God is giving you." Exodus 20:12 NLT

Prayer - Lord, I thank you for sparing my mother's life. Although she is not at one hundred percent health-wise, I, along with my family, am grateful for the reasonable portion of health and strength that she has. I pray that You continue to sustain her. We praise You for this day, understanding that You alone are worthy of all glory and honor. In Jesus' name, Amen!

Notes:

_____

_____

_____

_____

_____

_____

_____

_____

_____

_____

_____

_____

_____

_____

_____

_____

_____

_____

Concern For The Caregiver

It is the final day of my vacation. I am so grateful to have had the opportunity to take a real vacation this year. I have been fortunate not to have yet another conference doubling as a vacation and very little work interruptions. Thank you, Lord!

Although it is extremely hot here in Las Vegas (I'm writing this in August), I have had an enjoyable time. Today's weather forecast calls for the temperature to reach 105 degrees. Yikes!

As I sit on the balcony overlooking the gorgeous palm trees and other scenery that God has created, I can't help but tell God thank you. While my life is not quite what I had envisioned at this juncture, I am super, super blessed! Although my financial situation is not as prosperous as I would like, I thank God for favor that helps me manage and maintain. Most importantly, I am so thankful that my mother is still living and breathing and praying on this Earth, even if she is residing in a nursing home.

This morning I am reminded of Yolanda Adams' song which says, "I've been through many hard trials, through temptations on every hand. Though Satan tried to block me … He's kept me in the midst of it all!"

During this time away, I have come to realize how much I really needed this respite. My only regret is that I did not get away sooner. Things had gotten to the point where I was getting on my own nerves this past month.

I could tell that even my mother realized that I had become overwhelmed because she started telling me to reduce the frequency of my visits with her. She called a few times and expressed concern for me. I could tell that she was relieved a few days ago when I called to remind her that I was out of town.

Thank you, Lord, for helping me realize that getaways are necessary. I certainly do not want my mother to be concerned about my well-being when my charge is to care for her. The main takeaway is that if I do not take some time for myself, then I will eventually not be much help to the person for whom I am caring.

Scripture - *Then Jesus said, "Let's go off by ourselves to a quiet place and rest awhile." Mark 6:31 NLT*

Prayer - Lord, I thank You for bringing me to the realization that it is necessary to get away, not from the person for whom I am caring, but for my own benefit and self-preservation. Vacations serve as times of refreshing and renewal, which, in turn, will provide new energy and vitality to proceed with my responsibilities upon my return. I ask You to bless and keep my family, even when I am away. In Jesus' name. Amen!

Notes:

_____

_____

_____

_____

_____

_____

_____

_____

_____

_____

_____

_____

_____

_____

_____

_____

Decisions, Decisions

Saturday was a mentally taxing day. I was scheduled to work; however, when I called Mom, she told me that she felt terrible. She was exhibiting symptoms that would possibly lead her to the hospital. I was betwixt and between. Should I go to work or should I get on the road and head up to Hagerstown?

While I certainly do appreciate the support of family members who reside on the local side, I remain mindful of the fact that they have lives and responsibilities of their own. With that in mind, I try not to bother them unless necessary. I also try to make the trip up to handle Mom's affairs in person and see her myself, whenever possible.

In the end, I made the difficult decision to stay at work and check-in via telephone. Thankfully, Mom did not have to go to the ER. The doctor went into the nursing home and checked her out and was able to determine at least a temporary course of action.

I absolutely hate having to decide between working or making the drive to see her. The feelings of guilt that come along with being a caregiver are real. Work vs. travel, rest vs. visit, my bills vs. her bills, read my mail vs. her mail, my affairs vs. her affairs.

Lord, I truly ask and pray that You bring forth peace when the time comes to make these difficult situations.

Scripture - Thou wilt keep him in perfect peace, whose mind is stayed on thee: because he trusteth in thee. Isaiah 26:3 KJV

Prayer - Dear Lord, making decisions as a caregiver is not easy. I pray today that You will help me to know when to stay and when to go, when to rest and when to put forth the extra effort. Grant this day I pray, for discernment and stamina. Relieve guilt and self-doubt in Jesus' name. Amen!

Notes:

_____

_____

_____

_____

_____

_____

_____

_____

_____

_____

_____

_____

_____

_____

_____

_____

_____

_____

_____

I've Got Questions

1. Am I doing enough?
2. Does she know how much I love her?
3. Am I present enough so that the staff is attentive?
4. Should I move her closer to me?
5. How would my life be different if it weren't for this situation?

These are just a few of the questions that I have repeatedly asked myself. I did it so much that I felt myself becoming overwhelmed to the point of mental exhaustion.

At some point, we must stop second guessing ourselves. Otherwise, we will pull ourselves under. One thing I learned when attending a caregivers' workshop is that a depressed caregiver can become vengeful and neglect the very one for whom they care. Lord knows, I would never want to do that.

Let's be mindful that while self-reflection can be good, constant second guessing is not. In fact, it can be counterproductive.

As you engage in a time of reflection, redirect your thoughts and ask yourself the following:

1. As I care for my loved one, am I taking proper care of myself?
2. Do I have my personal affairs in order?
3. Do I have adequate insurance?
4. When was the last time that I took a vacation?
5. When was the last time that I actually took a day off to rest and relax?

Scripture - Create in me a clean heart, O God. Renew a loyal spirit within me. Psalms 51:10 NLT

Prayer - I come to You today, Lord, asking You to search me. Search my heart, Lord. I want to be sure that it is free and clear of feelings of anger at this situation. Check my motives. I don't serve in this capacity for money or any reason other than the fact that my loved one needs me. God, please settle and establish my mind on a firm foundation. Help me not to constantly second guess myself. Give me an assurance that You are indeed with us. Help me to answer the variety of questions that cross my mind from time to time. Make me better, Lord. This is my prayer, in Jesus' name. Amen!

Notes:

_____

_____

_____

_____

_____

_____

_____

_____

_____

_____

_____

_____

_____

_____

_____

_____

_____

_____

Applying Wisdom

On numerous occasions, people have asked me about moving my mother closer to me to help alleviate the hour and a half one-way drive. Truth of the matter is, I take my responsibilities of providing financial and custodial support very seriously. I also do my best to maintain open lines of communication with the nursing home staff. To that end, I would never want to make things easier for myself, yet more difficult for her. She and I spoke several times about moving her closer to me, and I told her it was totally up to her. I never wanted her to feel as though I were making her move away from the environment that she knew and loved.

When thinking of relocating my mother, I considered the fact that other family members, friends, her church family, and others whom she loves are closest to her. Most of them would not visit her as frequently, if she were moved to a facility that is over an hour away. In my opinion, it would be nearly impossible to replace decades of relationships that have been established.

I have known of other children who moved their aging parents. Moving them away from the familiar environment in many cases proved to be detrimental to their mental and physical health. In fact, in many instances, they declined quicker. This is not the case for all families. The main thing is that everyone must make the decision that's best for them, their family and their specific situation.

This is just an example of the difficult decisions that those of us who are entrusted with the well-being of another have to make. Whenever you are faced with a life-altering, life-defining decision, I encourage you to be sure that you are thinking clearly and deliberately. Do not allow your emotions or the physical state of tiredness to guide your decisions. Most importantly, seek wise counsel from those who you trust. Discuss the matter with your loved one, if possible. Above all else, seek the Lord! Ask Him for wisdom. He will lead and guide you in the right direction.

Scripture - For the Lord grants wisdom! From his mouth come knowledge and understanding. He grants a treasure of common sense to the honest. He is a shield to those who walk with integrity. He guards the paths of the just and protects those who are faithful to him. Proverbs 2:6-8 NLT

Prayer - Father, I come to You today asking that You lead me and guide me as I make critical decisions. I don't want to make any knee-jerk reaction type of decisions that will be harmful in the end. I speak Proverbs 3 over this situation. I am trusting You. I am not leaning to my understanding. I am acknowledging You. I thank You in advance for directing my paths. This is my prayer. in Jesus' name, Amen!

Notes:

_____

_____

_____

_____

_____

_____

_____

_____

_____

_____

_____

_____

_____

_____

_____

_____

_____

Memorial Sunday

I learned that my best friend is gravely ill in the hospital. I'm trying my best to keep it together because I had no idea that she was sick. Apparently, she went in for a minor procedure due to a prior surgery. She had a fever following the procedure; so she was kept overnight. She said that she didn't inform me of the procedure because she didn't want to worry me. Ugh! *Insert side eye here.*

I'm not going to lie. I was very upset that she did not inform me. In fact, I really wish people would cease and desist with secrecy under the guise of not worrying loved ones. In this case, it backfired big time! Most often, the results are that the issue they intended to avoid has now been compounded with angst and frustration.

How am I supposed to process my best friend having surgery, not telling me and now she's in ICU fighting for her life?

She told me over the phone that she would be released on Sunday. Still, I decided to stop by the hospital to visit after church. When I got there, I found out that she had taken a turn for the worse. She had been moved to the Intensive Care Unit and was on a ventilator to breathe.

Considering everything that has occurred with Mom, I could have simply passed out at the sight of my best friend laying there like that! This was so eerily similar to what happened to my mother just three years prior. I was so unprepared to see her breathing with assistance of a machine in addition to having numerous tubes and filters.

I got back in the car and had to pray before I made another move! I rebuked every demon and devil of death, complication and sickness before also praying over myself.

Prayer - God grant me the serenity to accept the things I cannot change, courage to change the things I can and the wisdom to know the difference.

Today, we take absolute authority over the enemy's plan to sap the life out of one of God's children. Let God's word be true and every man be a liar. We come against all complications and any further adverse turns in physical condition or negative doctor's reports.

We know our God to be a healer. We know Him to be a way maker; and we also know that even when WE are caught off guard, our GOD is never taken by surprise. Therefore, we rest in the perfect plan of our sovereign God. Lord, You said in Your word that healing is the children's bread. Therefore, we expect to see a manifestation thereof – healing! In Jesus' name, amen!

Notes:

_____

_____

_____

_____

_____

_____

_____

_____

_____

_____

_____

_____

_____

_____

_____

_____

_____

On The Upswing

After spending one week in the hospital, my mother has been released. Praise be to God!

Once again, the Lord exceeded my expectations! We needed a non-surgical solution to her situation; and the Lord granted just that! Moreover, He gave my mother favor with the attending physician. He would not release her from the hospital; although, the primary care physician at the nursing home tried to do so a few days ago. The attending physician refused and said that he would release her when he felt she was healthy enough. I am so grateful for physicians that see patients as people who need to be healed before releasing them from their care.

Caregiving brings a variety of emotions along the journey. I never want to be guilty of magnifying and remembering more challenges than triumphs. The fact of the matter is that God blesses with us with more victories than defeats. More opportunities are given than taken from us.

Oftentimes, we pray and praise the Lord when we need something. I take time today to salute the Lord for granting a specific request. Thank you, Lord!

Scripture - And we know that God causes everything to work together for the good of those who love God and are called according to his purpose for them. Romans 8:28 NLT

Prayer - Lord, I thank You for a tangible sign that things are working together for my good. Thank you for favor with those in key roles in caring for my loved one. Thank you so much for good days. Just as I seek You in prayer when I need something; today I want to take time to thank You for every answered request. I thank You for every dark day that You have turned into light, and for every down day that You have brought up. I will continue to put my trust in You. In Jesus' name, Amen!

Notes:

_____

_____

_____

_____

_____

_____

_____

_____

_____

_____

_____

_____

_____

_____

_____

_____

_____

It's All In Your Perception

A good friend lost her mom following a heart attack recently. Her loss prompted me to count myself among the blessed given the fact that my mother remains alive and reasonably well. While I know that Mom would absolutely love to be out and about more often, her ability to adapt to her situation has amazed me.

One thing that I really admire is that her adapting has not caused her to become complacent, rather to persevere without becoming bitter. Likewise, I've done my best during this leg of the journey not to complain about our family's current circumstance. While there could certainly be moments of "why us?" or "how could this be," I like, my mother, have opted to be content and count the fact that she is yet alive as a blessing from on high.

Although it has been five years since she became sick, we both look forward, by faith, to the day when Mom will be able to make the trip to my house for a visit. In the meantime, we maintain the perception and perspective that God remains good and that He is a keeper.

Scripture - But my God shall supply all your need according to his riches in glory by Christ Jesus. Philippians 4:19 KJV

Prayer - Dear Lord. Today, I first come to You on behalf of those who are mourning the loss of their loved ones. I pray that You comfort them during moments of hurt and loneliness. I ask, dear Lord, that You touch them during those difficult moments, and meet their every need.

I also want to take time to thank You that my family remains intact. I thank You so much that life continues. Today, I focus on maintaining the perception that the glass is half full, rather than half empty. My focus this day is on the fact that a reasonable portion of life, health and strength yet exists. For that I say, thank you!

Notes:

_____

_____

_____

_____

_____

_____

_____

_____

_____

_____

_____

_____

_____

_____

_____

_____

_____

Small Victories

I spoke with the lady in the Finance Department at Mom's nursing home today. She informed me that Mom's Medicaid has been frozen and they haven't been paid in three months!

I called the Department of Social Services to and spoke with the social worker. She stated that she needs proof that I have paid Mom's dental and vision insurance premiums. That isn't a problem because I had already sent the nursing home a copy of the cancelled check for payment to the insurance company.

The social worker also informed me that she needed the cash value of Mom's life insurance policy. The catch was that she needed it immediately, as in today; or I would be required to begin the application process over!

My stress level shot up 90 percent because Medicaid was the source of payment for Mom's nursing home stay and care. It also covered parts of her medical bills that aren't covered by Medicare. Losing coverage would have serious consequences.

Thanks be to God, I did have my mother's policy number and was able to call her insurance company. Most important was the fact that the customer service rep sent me the information that I needed within 30 minutes! I was able to meet what at first seemed to be an impossible deadline with hours to spare. Thank you Lord for favor!

Scripture - But thanks be to God who gives us the victory through our Lord Jesus Christ! 1 Corinthians 15:57

Prayer - Today, Lord, I thank You for small victories. I realize life is a marathon and not a 100-yard dash. With that in mind, I thank You for each checkpoint and each victory along the way. My request today is simple, yet in some ways complex. Lord, please grant me the ability to endure. Help me not to become so stressed and overwhelmed that I give up and forfeit the opportunity to experience the victories that You have pre-ordained for me. In Jesus' name, Amen!

Notes:

_____

_____

_____

_____

_____

_____

_____

_____

_____

_____

_____

_____

_____

_____

_____

_____

_____

_____

_____

Give Flowers Now

Today was perhaps one of the most meaningful and fulfilling days of my life. Glorious – that is the word that best describes this particular day. I was able to pull off the ultimate surprise for my mommy.

We had a surprise appreciation service for her at her church. I had only told her that one of her spiritual sons, Eric, who is a gospel artist, would be bringing his choir to the church to sing. I secured transportation to get her to the service, but I did not tell her that the service was to honor her.

Although it took a lot of coordination to pull things together, it worked out perfectly! Just as my cousin Troy wheeled Mom into the church, I announced that she was the honoree. The church was packed and the people gave her a standing ovation. The look on her face was absolutely priceless!

In addition to the people within the community, my cousins came from North Carolina and Pennsylvania. It was especially great that her niece, Mia who she had not seen in over 20 years, made it down for the surprise. Mom was so happy!

To top it off, the service was super blessed and as my close friend says, "in high gear." Eric and others from both the church and local community did wonderful tributes. Troy's tribute on behalf of our family brought everyone to tears as he explained that he knows the Lord today due to seeds that Mom had sown in his life when he was a boy. I even learned things about my mother that I had not previously known. She was a servant of God and the community for sure. She was a praying woman who loved others. She went out of her way to support single mothers.

Perhaps the most poignant moment was when my mom's best friend of over 40 years spoke. She shared that they had taken money from their personal accounts to help provide for single mothers during Thanksgiving and Christmas holidays. This was done while my mother was raising me alone. Just wow!

Witnessing the final outcome of the service left me feeling an immense sense of gratefulness. The Lord had laid it on my heart to have the surprise appreciation service one year earlier; however, I was unable to pull it off at that time. I am so glad that he spared her life to see how loved and appreciated she is. To me, it was an example of giving her flowers and accolades while she's yet alive to see and hear them. She talked about that service for months. My spirit says simply, "it is well."

Scripture - *Now we ask you, brothers and sisters, to acknowledge those who work hard among you, who care for you in the Lord and who admonish you. Hold them in the highest regard in love because of their work. Live in peace with each other. 1 Thessalonians 12:13 NIV*

Prayer - Lord, I thank You that delayed is not denied. Help us to give those whom we love their flowers while they are alive. May every caregiver find a way to bless their loved one, so they know with assurance that they are loved. This is my prayer. In Jesus' name, Amen!

Notes:

_____

_____

_____

_____

_____

_____

_____

_____

_____

_____

_____

_____

_____

_____

_____

_____

_____

_____

Simply Grateful

It's Thanksgiving and I'm grateful first and foremost that my mom is alive and well during this holiday. I'm especially thankful because we had a scare, which led to her spending two days in the hospital. Thanks be to God, it was a minor infection and not something more serious.

Although I've been to Hagerstown for the two past weekends and I'm exhausted physically, I'm heading up there for a visit today. My thought is that if God has kept her here, then she needs to see family especially during holidays. Considering the fact that there are those who feel as though they have nothing to be thankful for after losing loved ones, there are no sad songs or grudging visits here. There's nothing but gratefulness.

Scripture - *Give thanks to the lord, for he is good! His faithful love endures forever. Psalms 118:29 NLT; You gave me life and showed me your unfailing love. My life was preserved by your care. Job 10:12 NLT*

Prayer - Dear Lord, I come to You today thanking You that my family has remained intact this year. I thank You for the funeral that did not happen. I bless You for keeping my mother another year. As we leave this Thanksgiving weekend, I ask that You keep us both healthy. In Jesus' name, I pray. Amen!

Notes:

_____

_____

_____

_____

_____

_____

_____

_____

_____

_____

_____

_____

_____

_____

_____

_____

_____

_____

_____

_____

Check Your Outlook

Some days are great. Then, there are others when "woe is me" thoughts threaten to consume us. We know that the seasons of life bring change, but they also cause us to go through valleys and stand on mountains. There are also times when we feel as though we are barely moving or progressing.

In the Bible, James instructed us to count it all joy, but the reality is, doing so is more than a notion. In fact, it can be very difficult. Looking at our present circumstances, coupled with concerns about our future, can leave us feeling as though our joy has been depleted.

Alas, I have concluded that it really depends on the manner in which we view things. In other words, we need to check our outlook. Can you count it all joy when your savings account is nearly depleted? When the doctor tells you that your loved one will never get better? When you are drained from ripping and running? When your family is not supporting you? When your loved one is not easy to deal with?

Let's go back to our outlook. Counting life's tests and trials as joy is not fake. No, quite the contrary. It acknowledges what is currently taking place in our lives, while retaining hope that something positive will result even from the less than stellar life situations. It also, provides the peace and the stamina that are needed for us to hold on as we care for others.

Scripture - Dear brothers and sisters, when troubles of any kind come your way, consider it an opportunity for great joy. For you know that when your faith is tested, your endurance has a chance to grow. James 1:2-3 NLT

Prayer - Dear Lord, I come to You today acknowledging that I need Your help. I am asking You to help adjust my spiritual and emotional sight. I need an adjustment in the way that I view things. I want them to align with Your Word. Please help me to consider and count even the tests and trials in my life as opportunities for something positive to come forth. Help me to hold on, even when my faith is being tested. Most of all, Lord, help me to endure. I thank You in advance! In Jesus' name, Amen!

Notes:

_____

_____

_____

_____

_____

_____

_____

_____

_____

_____

_____

_____

_____

_____

_____

_____

_____

Living Through The End

Although I knew the end would come, I can truly say that living through the end of my mother's life was the most excruciatingly painful experience that I have *ever* endured.

Yes, I was aware that she had a relationship with the Lord and is in a better place. In fact, realizing that she was tired and depressed three months ago after her walking and mobility declined, I shifted my own prayers. I asked the Lord to take her if He was not going to heal her.

I knew how much Mom loved life and loved to get around, even while living at the nursing home. She regularly went from room to room, visiting other residents and loved it when the activities staff took them on outings to local restaurants. Once her health really declined, being more dependent on the nursing home staff simply depressed her. She had gotten to the point where she just would not eat much, if at all. She told me that she just did not feel hungry. Quite honestly, witnessing her decline further was very difficult for me as well.

Despite all of that, I still was not ready for her to leave me! I told my best friend on that dreaded night that I felt like an orphan, but she did not understand my statement. Having grown up without my biological father, then with an abusive step-father, Cindy was *it* for me. Losing her was super significant. Alas, all that I can do is trust God to bring me through this.

Getting that call from the doctor informing me that I needed to get to the hospital immediately was a game changer. Periodically, I envisioned that time and scenario. However, nothing came close to the real thing. I also pondered whether I would prefer to be there with her or not. In the end, that last 36 hours with her was priceless. I thank and praise God (even as I write through tears) for allowing my family and I to gather by Mom's bedside and play her favorite gospel and Motown songs.

Signing those hospice documents was surreal. Mom never had a terminal illness, so I never anticipated such. It was overwhelming and excruciating, but God gave me a level of peace through it. Living through the end is one of life's scenes that you will never be completely prepared for. However; the grace of God will carry you through, as has been the case countless other times. As I was told, you will never get over it, but you will make it through.

Scripture - Then you will experience God's peace, which exceeds anything we can understand. His peace will guard your hearts and minds as you live in Christ Jesus. Philippians 4:7 NLT

Prayer - Lord, I thank You for peace in my mind and emotions that goes beyond what I am able to understand. I lean on you for strength. In Jesus' name, Amen!

Notes:

_____

_____

_____

_____

_____

_____

_____

_____

_____

_____

_____

_____

_____

_____

_____

_____

_____

Great Is Your Reward

This journey has prompted me to ponder a few things along the way.

1. Why did God choose me to care for my mother?
2. Why didn't He equip me or train me for this?
3. Why didn't He give me siblings so that I could share this load?
4. Should I have left my job in order to be a better caregiver?

The Lord reminded me that He excels when I feel inadequate. He will pick up the slack. He will make up the difference. Although this journey has its moments of emptiness, the Lord has never left me in that state. He has helped me to fill the void.

Although there was no how-to manual for caregiving, I can honestly state that the Lord has led and guided me. He sharpened my discernment, strengthened my prayer life, and reinforced my walk with Him. He also led me to much needed resources at precisely the right time.

My mother and stepfather tried to have other children, but it did not work out. I realized that being the sole descendant of Cindy Mo was part of the plan and purpose. When all is said and done, we must bow to the will of God. I concluded that being an only child was part of the plan.

At one point, I asked my supervisor if I should take Family and Medical Leave because I was struggling with whether my job was being adversely impacted by my responsibilities with my mother. Living nearly two hours away from my mother made things more challenging. I realized that I was not as focused as I needed to be; and I did not want it to impact my job in the long-term. In the end, we concluded that FMLA was not necessary, as I had been fulfilling my obligations at work.

Alas, I realize that it was a sincere blessing to be able to care for my mother. I also hold fast to the word of God that we reap what we sow. My faith says that I *will* reap a harvest of blessings due to the seeds that I sowed over the last seven years caring for my mom. Those seeds were not always monetary. Sometimes, they were time and other times they were watered with tears, but the Lord will honor them with a harvest. Yes, I'm claiming it, and you should too!

Scripture - Honor your father and mother, as the LORD your God commanded you. Then you will live a long, full life in the land the LORD your God is giving you. Deuteronomy 5:16 NLT
For God is not unjust. He will not forget how hard you have worked for him and how you have shown your love to him by caring for other believers,[a] as you still do. Hebrews 6:10 NLT

Prayer – Lord, today I pause to thank you answering the questions that I have pondered in my heart. Likewise, I thank you in advance for the harvest that is coming. While I did not serve to receive, I am also aware that your word says we will reap what we have sown. I am confident that you will fulfill every promise that you made both to my family and to me personally. We stand in agreement and anticipation awaiting the manifestation thereof, in Jesus' name. Amen!

Notes:

_____

_____

_____

_____

_____

_____

_____

_____

_____

_____

_____

_____

_____

_____

_____

_____

_____

Reflections

As I reflect on my caregiving journey, several things come to mind.

Role reversal – I was not mentally prepared to have the strongest person in my world need me in this manner. That was extremely difficult. I don't think words can adequately convey how hard it is to have the one who gave you life now depend on you for most of their well-being. This is the part that I disliked most about caregiving. Knowing how I felt enabled me to imagine the emotional impact on my mother. With this in mind, I did my best to give her things before she would have to ask. For example, I was diligent with keeping money in her activities account, thus allowing her to retain some sense of independence.

Financial matters – The set-up of our social services system is somewhat insane. My mother had handled her business alone. She was on a ventilator and unable to speak when she got sick. The fact that five years of financial records had to be retrieved and submitted in order to qualify for assistance was a major hurdle when I first assumed this responsibility. Also, Medicare did not cover all her personal care needs. I am grateful that God blessed me to be able to cover the difference. Funds for clothing, personal care items and other necessities can be taken for granted until you are placed in this position.

Proper planning – I cannot stress enough the importance of proper end of life planning. If you are faced with the need to liquidate assets or doing a legal spend down, use the funds toward pre-burial needs. I secured a grave plot within a year of becoming a caregiver and made a sizeable deposit in addition to monthly payments. This alleviated a great deal of stress after my mother's passing. The majority of the burial expenses had already been covered, and I had adequate insurance for the rest.

Grateful – Caregiving in any capacity takes you on an emotional rollercoaster. However, it also brought me closer to my mother in a manner that I never believed possible. I can truly say that my life revolved around ensuring that Cindy was comfortable and as happy as possible.

When all was said and done, I am blessed to have been Cindy Mo's daughter. So many have told me that my mom was blessed to have me, but I beg to differ. As I type this through tears, I can say that *I* was blessed to have *her*. Her life and legacy of serving God and His people, in addition to prayer is so ingrained within me. She made me the woman that I am today. #CelebratingCindyMo #CindyMosDaughter

Scripture - Always be joyful. Never stop praying. Be thankful in all circumstances, for this is God's will for you who belong to Christ Jesus. 1 Thessalonians 5:16-18 NLT

Prayer - Today, Lord, I thank You for the time to reflect. As I do so, I can truly say that my good days have outweighed my bad days. Through every mountain, every valley, every storm and test, You have been an ever-present help. Thank you for that, Lord! Thank you for this leg of the journey. I have learned so much about myself, others, and You, Lord. You have shown Yourself to be great in my life; and I am simply thankful. In Jesus' name, Amen!

Notes:

_____

_____

_____

_____

_____

_____

_____

_____

_____

_____

_____

_____

_____

_____

_____

_____

_____

Thank you

To my Heavenly Father: thank you so much for loving me and for choosing me for this great work. I love you Lord!

To my family, and friends who are like family: Please know that I appreciate every road trip that you took with me, every visit, every trip to the hospital or nursing home, every gift, every meal you prepared, every prayer you prayed, and every time that you lent a listening ear.

To my Pastors Bishop Alfred & Dr. Susie Owens, Bishop T. Cedric Brown & Lady Bobette Brown, Presiding Elder Darin Mency, and Bishop Sterling V. Porter and the Greater Mount Calvary Holy Church and King's Apostle Church families, Dr. Mary Breaux Wright, and my Zeta Phi Beta Sorors: thank you for every prayer that you prayed, every word of encouragement, and every kind sentiment. They helped keep me on my feet when my strength was weak.

To Charron Monaye and Pen Legacy Publishing: thank you for all that you have done to help me share this message.

To everyone who encouraged and supported me as I worked to fulfill this God-given assignment.

About the Author

Teraleen R. Campbell is a native of Hagerstown, Maryland and currently resides in the Washington, DC metropolitan area. She is a member of Greater Mt. Calvary Holy Church in Washington, DC which is pastored by Bishop Alfred Owens, Jr. and Dr. Susie Owens. In addition to serving in the ministry, she is a certified coach. One who knows the worth of prayer, Teraleen loves to intercede for others. She serves as lead intercessor each month for the Sisters Prayer Circle which is sponsored by Sisters 4 Sisters, Inc.

She became a member of Zeta Phi Beta Sorority, Inc. at the University of Maryland, where she conducted her undergraduate studies. She has numerous leadership positions in the organization, most recently serving as National Co-Director of Marketing. Her ministry extends to Zeta, as she now serves on the Interdenominational Ecumenical Team. Teraleen authored the sorority's Centennial Prayer, has facilitated the Global Day of Prayer and co-authored the Faith of Our Founders Devotional Book.

Her community involvement includes the Prince George's County March for Babies Committee and Maryland Legislative Agenda for Women. She is Immediate Past President of a local club for Toastmasters International. Teraleen is a tireless advocate against domestic violence engaging elected officials, supporting survivors, conducting workshops and sitting on panels that address this issue. Southern Management Corporation, the March of Dimes and the American Red Cross have recognized her for her involvement and service to the community. Additionally, she was named Sorority Woman of the Year during the annual Sister-to-Sister Sorority Luncheon, hosted by Taylor Thomas of WHUR Radio. She also was recognized by her sorority, having been inducted into Zeta's Maryland State Hall of Fame in 2016. She was named one of the DC Metropolitan area's 100 Phenomenal Women in 2015. She is a contributing author of Behind the Scenes of a Phenomenal Woman, which was released in 2018.

With Christ as her focus, friend and guide, Minister Campbell's earnest desire is to be a vessel fit for the Master's use. (2 Timothy 2:21)

CPSIA information can be obtained
at www.ICGtesting.com
Printed in the USA
FFHW011945220119
50093328-54970FF